Coming out of the Darkness

Sky Munson

BookLeaf
Publishing

India | USA | UK

Presentation by *BookLeaf Publishing*

Web: www.bookleafpub.com

E-mail: info@bookleafpub.com

ISBN: 9789363300859

First edition 2024

Word Dump

SometimesMyBrainIsTooFullOfWordsToBeAbl
eToStringThemIntoAnyCoherentSentenceSoIJus
tSitInSilenceWhileMyMindSoundsLikeAStadiu
mFullySoldOutAndBustingAtTheSeamsWithPe
opleAndAnyoneAroundAssumesThatIHaveNoth
ingToSayWhileISitWishingICouldPlugMyBrainI
ntoASpeakerOrAMonitorScreenJustToGetMyTh
oughtsOutOfMyBrainAndFinallyBeHeardAndU
nderstood

Life in all Sizes

2

Overwhelming vastness and
unending beauty in the
forests and mountains and oceans

Tiny lives that make a difference in
the running of the world in the
bees and bugs and birds

I love all of the life that our world
provides and supports day to day,
big and small and in between

(big) Little Her

Little girl, so precious and innocent
hold tight to your gentleness
your soft loving towards life.
Little girl, life hits hard and will
knock you down until you are
bleeding and scarred and alone.
Little girl, know you'll be okay
know your gentleness holds
great strength and power.
Little girl, hold on tight because at the end
of all the battles and brawls
life is just so beautiful.
Little girl, I know you will bloom
you and life will be beautiful again
when little her is big

Picking upy Pieces

When life breaks you down
and tears you apart,
when you're in a million pieces
looking at your shattered heart

Remember that you are in charge
of what pieces you keep,
so look around at what is here
you dont have to dig deep

Each big event that feels like
like a major explosion
takes away and creates new pieces
all you need is devotion

Take the time you need
to sift through the pieces here,
making the decision of what to keep
and what to clear

Romanticizing Sunday

5

Wake up quietly, no alarms
Eggs and potatoes cooking in the kitchen
Sitting on the patio, cool quiet air
Afternoon family adventures
Memories made of peace
Early dinner and a walk to watch
the sunset
Falling asleep in each others arms as we talk
about our past and our future

Little Things

Moonlight on my face
a quiet sunset
Rain on the windshield
two bugs dancing
There's so many small things, quiet things,
that are big breathtaking things,
that make me think of you
and the memories you have burned into me
A reassuring hug will never be just a hug,
a gentle hand on my leg never just a touch,
your gaze will never be just eye contact
because every little thing
is our love

Fed

I once said I was starving
but not for food, and no one understood.
But now I am fed.
Avocado and egg hash browns, and a ride to
work in the morning.
A packed lunch of leftovers, and checking in
how my days going in the afternoon.
Homemade alfredo and cooking for me after
working all day in the evenings.
I wasn't starving for food, I needed my soul fed.

Eyes

The way you look at me
scoops me up off my feet
and into another universe
The depth is terrifying
but there is something else there
that makes it feel safe and welcoming
The way you look at me
makes my knees weak
and my confidence strong
The way every color imaginable
exists in your eyes
but you still think mine are beautiful
Your eyes are my favorite adventure

Healing

I wish you knew how your place in this life
is so healing
your words, your actions, your desires
are all so healing

Too many people rush through life
unknowingly, unintentionally, unrepairably
hurting people. Then leave them
when they're broken down

You found me, the scarred mess that i was, and
still recognized my soul. Scooped
me up like a feather, and whisked me away
to a safe life. A warm life. A quiet life.

Your every day, simple actions
are my brain rewiring, life changing, heart
healing moments. So natural to you
that you don't even seem to know

your place in this life is so healing

Define my Feelings

I
LOVE (an intense feeling of deep affection)
ADORE (love and respect someone deeply)
CHERISH (protect and care for someone
lovingly)
APPRECIATE (recognize the full worth of)
Admire (regard an object, quality, or person with
respect or warm approval)
RESPECT (a feeling of deep admiration for
someone or something elicited by their abilities,
qualities, or achievements)
YOU

I went to the dictionary looking to define my
feelings for you, but this still feels its only
scratching the surface

Define my Feelings (pt 2)

Outside of a dictionary
words don't mean anything
we give them meaning
the way we assign names to people
Outside of a dictionary, my feelings for you are
floating amoung the twinkling stars,
exploring every corner seeing every tree,
feeling my past disappear,
and watching my future bloom,
My feelings for you are
the first rays of sunshine on my face,
birds singing with not a care in the world,
the green of thawing spring and
cozy nights cuddled with a book by a fire
My feelings for you can't be defined
by words, only feelings

Missing Person

There was a missing person until recently.
There was never any physical description
or a face sketch given.
There were never any leads or tips.
only a hole, a void. an ache and longing, for
someone with an unknown name.
The moment we found each other and
everything fell into place making sense,
no one was missing.
Everything was in its place. And i wonder, this
entire time who was actually the
missing person

Love at First (sight isn't real)

13

I didn't fall in love with you when I saw you. It
took more than a photo and eye contact.
but
the moment we met, your soul energy got near
mine and it felt like home. Call it
love at first recognition, the second you meet
someone who feels as though you've known
them your entire life.
Love at first touch, not a moment of discomfort
or awkwardness only wanting to be close
Love at first energy mesh, once you know you're
meant to be together and it's painful to be apart
I've loved you since the start, love at first.

Gentle Giant

Tall and towering above me, but always my
equal
Giant hands, patiently waiting for my little
fingers to be in between
Strongest muscles I've ever seen, for adventuring
or lifting me into the best embrace
Some days I'm still stunned by this giant, this
strong muscle man. I was once made to believe I
was small and inherently weak and less than;
only to be gifted this gentle giant, who only
wants to protect and cherish me.

My Love

When I call you my love
it is not just a pet name
or an empty statement
When i call you my love
I am reminding you that you have my heart
when you leave the house for the day
When i call you my love
I am thanking the universe that you are
MY love
When i call you my love
I am trying my best to put into words
that you are all my love, everything I love,
all the love I've wished for, all in a person

Camp Views

up in the mountains
laying in a small hammock
together, always

Family

17

count them; one, two, three
finally a family
the happiest end

Goodbye

18

never enough time
i said goodbye on the floor
life's been empty since

Grief

In the first moments
time freezes, nothing feels real
while my brain rushes to process
I don't even know how I feel
But then it eventually hits
like a deadly tidal wave
this is real, this is happening,
they are gone and cant be saved
Only then does my body let out any emotion,
in the most pain filled scream
I plead with the sky that I'll wake up
and it'll all be a terrible dream

but days go on and I haven't woken
from a nightmare where you're not here
I just do my best to keep keeping on
and share the memories that are most dear

To my Dog

My Kaipo, oh how I miss you.
hard days i miss you selfishly,
but lately i miss you selflessly.
My Kaipo Pipe-o, how I miss you.
everything used to be unpromising,
but now most days are heartwarming.
My PoPo, I miss you.
but I know you had part in sending me him,
now my unending love will never dim.

Missing You

21

On good days I miss you
On hard days i miss you
On days i am outside on adventures
On days i can't possibly leave my bed
Days i see things that remind me of you
Days there's no evidence you were here
Days i see you in the sun
Days i feel you in the air
I miss you every moment
of every day